Heal Me

Heal Me

IN THE SHADOW OF PAIN, CRADLED BY THE LIGHT

KHIN LAY MAW

Cover design by: © Khin Lay Maw, 2026
Cover illustrations by: © Khin Lay Maw, 2026
Interior illustrations by: © Khin Lay Maw, 2026
Text by: © Khin Lay Maw, 2026

Publisher: Khinspirations Creative Designs LLC
For permissions or inquiries, contact: khinspirationsauthor@gmail.com

First Edition
Paperback ISBN: 979-8-9993297-1-4
EBook ISBN: 979-8-9993297-5-2
Hardcover ISBN: 979-8-9993297-3-8

Printed in the United States of America

Dedication

I am dedicating this book to you!

If you are going through a difficult time in your life, I hope that this book can become a companion to gently remind you of the beautiful healing presence of the Creator.

Acknowledgement

I would like to thank the Creator for granting me wisdom and guiding me on my journey. As I have navigated different life experiences, I have found joy in sharing what I have learned to create and pass down what I hope will be a beautiful legacy that will last for many generations to come. I am forever thankful to the Creator.

I am also deeply grateful for my family, which has served as a beautiful support system offering guidance, encouragement, and love. My parents, my husband, and my child have all been unwavering pillars of support throughout my life. I deeply love and appreciate these souls. I also wish to extend my gratitude to my beautiful sisters, nieces and brothers-in-law. They hold permanent places in my heart. To the relatives, friends, teachers, and mentors whose influence has been instrumental in shaping my journey, I also extend my heartfelt appreciation.

Finally, my special thanks to all my readers. You are the heart of this book. Thank you!

It was through the collective contributions of everyone in my life and in this world that I have come to embrace the beauty that surrounds me. Thank you for allowing me to express my deepest gratitude!

Foreword

Poetry, for me, is a beautiful way to express my thoughts and emotions in a tangible form. It allows me to express myself to others in ways that are gentle and compassionate.

Poetry has always been a natural part of me. The words seem to arrive effortlessly, flowing through me with a quiet ease. Writing poems feels like something I was simply meant to do—an instinctive way of expressing what lives in my heart.

In the moments when I write or read a poem, I feel completely present. Much like painting a canvas, the process of writing poetry draws me in so deeply that time and space fade away. I become immersed in the beauty of expression, in the quiet joy of creating something meaningful.

From the knowledge and wisdom I have gathered through my life experiences, I am able to share these verses in the form of short reflections with the hope that someone, somewhere can benefit from them.

Poetry helps me reflect the beauty of this world and the depth of the life experience. My sincere hope is that these poems can

bring you new perspective in your life and give you the strength
and courage you need to navigate your own life experiences with
love, compassion and wisdom.

Introduction

The moments in which we face challenges in our lives can feel painful, long and lonely. Sometimes we wonder if anyone can understand our pain, but truly, only those who have gone through similar experiences can step into our shoes and see our perspective. Even then, people are not always from the same background and have not had similar life experiences, so they cannot fully comprehend our point of view. They can only try to make us feel better with some guidance based on what they know and have learned from their own life experiences.

When we see the challenges we face as mountains, we cannot see beyond them. Each new and frightening challenge seems to be the biggest, most overwhelming problem, and anything beyond that seems impossible to reach. Maybe it is because we are standing at the base of that mountain and looking up at its peak, but we must remember that we have climbed many mountains in the past, and we were able to succeed then because of hope, faith, and trust in ourselves.

When we feel that we do not have enough hope, faith, or trust in ourselves, we try to find them in others, who are also either at the base of their own mountain or in the process of climbing one, they will not be able to spare much help to us. So, we need to place our trust in the Divine, who created the mountains. The Creator is the ultimate source of light and love. If we are looking for hope, we have to place our trust in the Creator, for the Creator is the one who can move mountains for us.

I wrote this book in the hopes of leaving a lasting legacy for that those who are going through adversity. I hope that you can find a friend in its pages during times of shadow. In these short reflections, I hope that you, the reader, can experience the journey of pain and adversity transforming into hope, trust and faith in the Creator. In the times of shadow in your life, this book is a gentle reminder that you can discover yourself and place your hopes in the Creator.

None of us are alone in what we go through. The Creator's love is cradling us every step of the way. Each of us are held and loved. You are enough, and are worthy, simply because you exist. No other requirements are needed for you to be worthy and enough. It is that simple. You are not defined by your achievements, talents, skills, or qualities. You are worthy and loved by the Creator for who you are, as a pure soul, and anything you do is just an expression of the Creator's love and compassion. There is no need to earn validation, seek approval, or prove your worth to others when you are whole and complete. It is absolutely beautiful when you create from a place of love, because gentle compassion towards others is the most important thing you can bring to the people around you.

I dedicate this book to you in the hope that it can be by your side to show you that you, too, can overcome these difficult moments, and to help you find your strength, hope, and renew your faith in the Creator.

Lost in the Shadows

I pleaded
O my Lord
help me
help me

when they broke the news
my first thought
was not for myself
but *what will happen
to my child now?*

I sat down on the bed
my heart was so heavy
that the mattress
sank a little
in sympathy

I cried an ocean of tears
I visualized my entire life
past, present and future
in sixty seconds

I looked up to the sky
and asked *why?*

more like
why me?

I pleaded
O my Lord
guide me
guide me

I kept staring at the board
in that room

I read the same lines
like the name of the nurse
for the hundredth time

I thought maybe
I could write them
more neatly

the names on the board kept changing
except mine

I did not like that board

I kept staring at the curtain
in that room

I thought I could design a better one
with brighter and happier colors

I thought when I get well
maybe I will design a nice one
so that newcomers
can have a happier curtain
to look at

I did not like that curtain

I kept staring at the clock
in that room

the slowest clock
that ever existed

it took an eternity
to go from one second
to the next

I felt like bringing it down
from the wall
and spinning its hands
so that time would go faster

I did not like that clock

I kept staring at the painting
in that room

I have analyzed
every single detail of it

it felt like it was trying
to make me happy

instead, I thought I was making it happy
with my company

what a lonely painting
it sits and waits for newcomers

it tries to make friends with
each person who comes to that room

I did not like that painting

I kept looking out the window
in that room

it felt like a painting of dreams
the people outside were
walking, running, riding bikes

how joyful those people seemed
in that
painting of dreams

how I wished I could also
be a part of that dream

I did not like that window

I kept playing with the remotes
in that room

one moved my bed
up and down

one turned on the television
but I was not interested

it seemed like
playing with remotes was
the only fun I could have

I did not like those remotes

I kept looking at my child's photo

it was time for my medicine
when even the birds were still asleep

I kept looking at my child's photo

even the rooster was not awake yet
but I had to make peace with the silence

I kept looking at my child's photo

I missed those eyes and that smile
the tenderness of hugs and kisses

the only thing I loved
was that photo

I pleaded
O my Lord
inspire me
inspire me

how I kept wishing
I was home

holding my child
in my arms

sleeping
next to my child

telling my child
beautiful stories

I kept looking for
someone or something
in the corridor

there were no flowers
no happy things
nothing exciting to look at

I thought
when I am well
I will bring some flowers
for my friends to look at

I pleaded
O my Lord
restore me
restore me

oh, how I missed
my comfortable bed
my soft pillow

the comfort of waking up
in my beautiful room
next to my loved one

the joy of seeing sunshine
pouring through the windows
hearing the sounds of lovely birds
and looking at green trees

I felt so lonely
in what I was going through
that I even made friends
with a dot
on an imaging device

the dot was quite friendly
it accompanied me
I felt loved
I felt that I was not alone
in that moment

but even the dot could not
be there for me
always

family and friends
came and visited

but they, too, had to leave
at the end of the day

no one could be
with me
always

oh, how I missed
my loved ones

and their laughter
and their joy
and their love
and their warmth

as I walked down the corridor
I heard friends hurting
in different rooms

their pain wanted to befriend my pain
we heard their call
my pain and I

I wanted to be there to tell them
they would be okay
and that we would get through this

my mind knocked on their doors
and asked *how I can help?*

but my body stood there
where it was
needing assistance to walk

my mind and my body
both of us could not be
in the same place
at the same time

I pleaded
O my Lord
carry me
carry me

I heard the same prayer
from the hearts
of my friends

Found by Grace

each room is filled with
a similar sorrow
and a similar regret

I pleaded
O my Lord
change me
change me

why did we not remember?

we are all flowers
hoping for the Creator's rain

why did we not remember?

we are all embraced
by the Creator's love

why did we not remember?

we are all surrounded
by the Creator's healing light

why did we not remember?

we are all strengthened
through the hope in the Creator

why did we not remember?

we are all consoled
in the Creator's embracing arms

why did we not remember?

we are all uplifted
by the grace of the Creator

why did we not remember?

we are all nurtured
by the care of the Creator

why did we not remember?

we are all restored
in the compassion of the Creator

I pleaded
O my Lord
bless me
bless me

if we try to comprehend
the Creator's love
with our logical minds
and our five senses
we will have difficulty
understanding it

the Creator's love must be felt
with our hearts
and be connected to
with our souls

imagine yourself
being surrounded
by the Creator's pure love

imagine yourself
being surrounded
by the most
unconditional love

imagine yourself
being cradled
by the
gentlest care

imagine yourself
being surrounded
by the purest light of all

imagine yourself
being protected
in the same way
you were protected
by your mother's womb

you did not need to justify
that protection
through talent or service
you were simply held
safe
for months

there
in your mother's womb
gently floating
in embryonic fluid
fed by the umbilical cord
simply because you were alive

so how can we question
the love of the Creator?

how can we question
the purity of that love?

how can we forget
that the Creator's love
is the most powerful thing that exists?

in the divine love
and protection
of the Creator,
we find peace
we find acceptance
we find hope
we find strength
and we trust

you are no longer
a tiny human
standing at the base of
a gigantic mountain
looking up
and feeling overwhelmed

now you are a giant
holding that mountain
in your hands
what a tiny problem
to have overcome

you now have the tools
strength
courage
hope
faith
love
light
and trust

you have transformed

PART THREE

Walking in His Light

when I left that place
my mind wished my friends
farewell

no, I was not sad to leave
but I was not thrilled either
instead I was grateful

knowing that many would stay
in that place
feeling the same

knowing that many would come
to that place
feeling the same

I just hope that
during their stay
they can also find
the healing presence
of the Creator

I hope their stay is not too long

that they don't need
to read the same board
over and over again

or be annoyed
by the curtain's design

or feel like forcing
the hands of that clock to turn

or wish that painting
was more friendly

or look wistfully out that same window
beyond which all the joy exists

or play with those remotes
that are fairly boring

or longingly stare at a beautiful photo
of their loved ones

or walk, assisted, through the loneliest
    corridors
without being able to help others

I hope their stay is not too long

I wonder why
we do not remember our Lord
when we are well

but we call out to Him
when we are in need

I wonder why
our love is so conditional

we call Him
when we need Him

we remember Him
only when He can help us

we think of Him
when there is nothing left
to think of

why is our love
so conditional?

yet our Lord still
helps us

during those times
we do not ask the question
why?

more like
why me?

I pleaded
O my Lord
forgive me
forgive me

if there was a purpose
to this illness
I feel maybe it was
to make me kneel down
to find my hope
to gather my strength
to rise in courage
to teach me love
to make me well
and to spread that love

the unconditional love
of the Creator

if we are souls inside bodies
our bodies are
reflections of the divine design
entrusted with purpose by the Creator

our pure souls reside in them
our gentle souls pray through them

so, we need to treat our bodies
with love and respect

when we are well,
we must remember
that our body is
a gift from the Creator

when we are well,
we must remember that
our health is
a gift from the Creator

when we are well,
we must remember that
we still need our Creator
every step of the way

when we are well,
we must remember that
life is a precious gift
each breath is sacred

when we are well
we can appreciate
mornings
people
messes
children
busy schedules
breath
heartbeats
waking up
existence itself

we are always in need
of the love and guidance
of the Creator

we are always in need
of the healing presence
of the Creator

all the sustenance
we receive
the good health
we have
all the wealth
we own
all the love
we are granted

none of that
was given
so that we could forget
the One who gave
and remember Him only
when we lose it all

only when we remember each day
to thank the Creator
can we prosper
in that abundance

for any parent,
the hardest part of
any illness is
the pain of not being
able to hold, hug and kiss
their children

our families
our spouses
our children
our friends
our relatives
are all gifts
cherish them

they are not the chaos
in our lives
they are the intended noise
in our lives
we need that noise
we need that love
we need that support
we need those gifts
cherish those noises

because when that noise
is absent
it can get pretty quiet
too quiet
you may not like it
you may miss it

I pleaded
O my Lord
heal me
heal me

heal the malady
in my heart
which forgot about you
when I was well

heal the malady
in my love
which was so conditional
and in need of approval

heal the malady
in my soul
which did not allow me
to serve you
when I was able

heal the malady
in my mind
for I did not think of you
when I was full of joy

heal the malady
in my body
that is now stopping me
from kneeling in front of you

heal the malady
in me

in my heart
in my love
in my soul
in my mind
in my body

instill light in me
instill love in me
instill trust in me
instill hope in me
instill strength in me
instill courage in me

make me pure
make me loving
make me truthful

make my mind
peaceful
make my heart
gentle
make my love
unconditional

I pleaded
O my Lord
fill me
fill me

this tunnel
may feel
long, lonely and dark

but as you search for
the light
at the end of it

remember that
you are always holding
the Light of the Creator

you can brighten
the entire tunnel,
your whole journey,
with Creator's love and light

you are never alone
Creator is always with you
every step of the way
loving you
guiding you
uplifting you
teaching you

you just need to
remember
to say

heal me

I am forever grateful
for Your unconditional love

it is my turn
to love You
unconditionally

I pleaded
O my Lord
lead me
lead me

Afterword

Each life experience teaches us lessons about ourselves and makes us wiser and stronger. While we are experiencing that hardship, it may seem impossible to get through, but that is when our faith in the Creator is being tested.

Throughout the hardships in life, we have to believe that we can persevere, and we must keep faith that the Creator will help us make it through. That faith will strengthen us and help us move forward.

Mindset is one of the key factors to face challenges with love and compassion for yourself. Staying motivated can feel hard in the beginning, but maintaining a positive mindset is important.

It is my purest and sincere hope that you can navigate your life experiences with love and compassion for yourself, as well as hope and trust in the Creator. I hope that this book can provide you with a light in the darkness to guide you from sorrow, fear, and doubt towards hopefulness, courage and strength.

Sometimes, we underestimate our own strength and resilience, but we can find reminders of our abilities by connecting with the strength and compassion of the Creator. We need to be receptive to the strength, love and kindness of the Creator to become strong and hopeful again.

I hope that this book helps you to find a place of love and gentleness for yourself and helps you navigate your life experiences with renewed strength and a more positive outlook. When you look back at your previous life experiences, you will find the version of you who overcame them to be stronger and wiser than the younger you. You will know that these experiences shaped you into who you are today. You are a beautiful human being and you always will be regardless of what happens to you. Always remember that you are worthy and enough because the Creator loves you.

I believe in you. Now, it is the time to believe in yourself.

About the Author

Khin Lay Maw is an author and artist who has a deep passion for finding meaning in life's experiences. Through poems inspired by the lessons she's gathered on her journey, she hopes to offer gentle inspiration to others—encouraging transformation, healing, and a deeper connection to oneself and the Creator.

Khin is a devoted wife and loving mother who resides in the United States, where her heart is rooted in family, creativity, and compassion. Her writing is a soft invitation to find kindness in everyday moments, and to help nurture a more loving and mindful world.

In the quiet spaces of her life, Khin finds joy in painting, meditation, learning new things, exploring nature, and capturing its beauty through photography.

Connect with her directly through her website to learn more and stay in touch: www.khinspirations.com

instagram.com/khinspirations

facebook.com/khinspirations

tiktok.com/khinspirations

youtube.com/khinspirations

threads.com/khinspirations

The Sacred Bloom

A GRACEFUL UNFOLDING OF HEALING AND WHOLENESS

"A poetry collection made for women—those who are blooming, transforming, healing, or simply becoming."

The Sacred Bloom is a collection of soul-touching, heartfelt poems that explores a graceful inner journey through life experiences in which love, adversity, motherhood, healing and self-discovery are profoundly unfolded petal by petal, leading to a full bloom of the self.

Each verse intricately portrays raw emotions, describing the soul's journey as it evolves from the purity and innocence of youth to the enlightenment that comes with womanhood and growth.

This collection includes nearly 60 works of poetry poised to resonate deeply with the reader's soul in diverse ways, and each is accompanied by beautiful floral illustrations.

Whether you are on a journey of self-improvement and personal growth, or seeking inner peace and transformation, this collection is perfect for you or a loved one.

Whispers of The Soul

A COLORING JOURNEY INTO STILLNESS, LIGHT, AND GENTLE PRESENCE

"A gentle coloring experience
for moments of calm, reflection, and simply being."

Whispers of The Soul is a calming and reflective coloring book created as a companion to *Heal Me*. Rooted in the same emotional and spiritual landscape, this collection of abstract floral illustrations invites you into a quiet space of stillness, where expression flows softly and without expectation.

Each design carries an organic, fluid quality—echoing themes of surrender, healing, and inner unfolding. As you bring color to the pages, you are gently encouraged to slow down, to breathe, and to be present with whatever thoughts or feelings arise. There is no right or wrong way to engage with these illustrations—only an invitation to meet them as you are.

This coloring journey is not about perfection, but about presence. It offers a simple, grounding practice that can be returned to in moments of reflection, restlessness, or quiet seeking. Whether paired with the poetry or experienced on its own, it becomes a space where the mind softens and the heart can settle.

Whispers of The Soul is a gentle reminder that even in stillness, there is movement, and even in quiet, there is light.